How to Deal with Difficult People

Easy Strategies for Dealing with People
You Can't Stand!

By
The Customer Service
Training Institute

Other Customer Service Training Manuals from The Customer Service Training Institute

Customer Service Basics

Conflict Resolution

Service Recovery Skills

How to Interact with All Kinds of Customers

Great Customer Service Over the Phone

Customer Service for Frontline Personnel

Enhancing the Customer Experience

Customer Service Training for Service Technicians

Customer Service Training for the Hospitality Sector

Customer Service Training for Health Care Professionals

Customer Service Excellence for Security Officers

Safety in the Workplace

"Sometimes something difficult can be made easier with the right approach and a little patience"

Table of Contents

Introduction

Life would be so much easier if everyone were nice and easy going like you and I. However, life just doesn't go like that. Unfortunately there are a group of people who seem like the entire purpose of their lives is to make our lives miserable.

Fortunately for us, these people are a minority in this world even though it might not seem like that to us at the time. The vast majority of people are nice and friendly and will be an important asset to our lives in one form or another.

The bad thing is that we cannot avoid those difficult people all the time. We have to work with them, sometimes we find ourselves related to some of them, or we are forced to deal with them in order to get something we want in life. So we cannot avoid them; we must learn how to deal with them.

Even though difficult people are not often considered positive parts of our lives, this book will deal with positive things we can do to make dealing with difficult people as easy and painless as possible. We will not dwell in the negative as that does no one any good.

This book is all about getting results. The results we need or desire in life in order to live the lifestyle we have chosen for ourself. It is not about putting anyone down, getting revenge over someone who gave us a hard time or even taking advantage over a difficult person. It is about getting results and only getting results.

It is our intention to educate you on how to interact with difficult people, how to reason with them and eventually co-exist with them. Take it from me, you can do this. There are reasons for everyone's actions and personalities. Very often understanding people is the most important step in relating and interacting with them.

That being said, this book is not a touchy feely book on bonding with human emotions or anything like that. We are not out to cure someone or to get a difficult person to have an epiphany or anything like that. Again, this is all about results.

With all of this in mind, let's get started!

How to Use This Book

This book contains a ton of information. Every part of this book will have some relevance for some people reading this book. Otherwise, we would have left that material out. There is no filler and no long stories about mean and difficult people we have cured through patient effort and advanced techniques.

This book is all about getting results and nothing else.

With that in mind it is important to let everyone know that not everything in this book might be relevant to you and your situation. We all know different types of individuals and some of these may fall into certain profiles while others may not.

So the first thing we must do is have some kind of idea who we are dealing with. The beginning parts of this book will deal in general terms about the effects difficult people have in our lives while the remainder of the book will deal with different approaches and topics that will help you deal with these people.

To help the new reader who opens this book get help immediately, you can go to the chapter headings to find descriptions as to what is covered in each chapter. So you can skip ahead to something you might need help with right now. So instead of reading chapters 1-15, you can get straight into chapter 16 which is what you think you need right now.

This has been proven to be a very effective way of training and learning especially for people who need help right away. Because of this format, you might find some things repeated throughout this book. This is not a mistake or copywriter error. Instead, it is to provide background information that is critical to the topic of discussion. So if you start on Chapter 16 and there is something that is critical to understanding that chapter, it will be included there to make sure you understand.

Whether you start at chapter 1 or skip ahead to any other part of the book, I strongly urge you to go back at some point and read through the entire book. It's not all that long and even though you think you might already know something, or feel it is not needed by you, still read through that chapter. It just might make you think about something a little bit differently.

Even though we already touched on this in the introduction, it is important to understand that there are probably topics and discussions in this book that do not pertain to you or your life right now. You must be aware of everything in your life so that you know what pertains to you and what doesn't.

Blissfully unaware or clueless is not a good way to go through life.

As you read this book, stop after every chapter and determine if what you have just read pertains to you and your life. If it does, figure out how to implement what you just read in your life NOW! Knowledge only has value in your life if you use it. If you learn something but never use the knowledge, it does you little good.

Implement some of the processes and approaches in this book and monitor the results you get. If you make the right choices you should see positive results. But if something doesn't get the results you are looking for, learn to adapt. Make changes and monitor those changes carefully.

That also means figuring out some way to measure your successes or failures. This is usually very easy. You change something and if the person you are dealing with is less dangerous or difficult from that point on, you are heading in the right direction. But if things should stay the same or even get worse, it's time to make mid course corrections and try something else.

I find it amusing when people tell me they read a book or took a course but it didn't do them any good. When I ask them how they implemented or used their new found knowledge, they tell me they didn't really change anything. Yet they expected different results.

One thing in life usually can be counted on. That is that if you do nothing, nothing will change.

If you want different results, you have to change your responses or your actions in order for those results to change.

Someone once said the definition of insanity is to do the same things over and over yet expect different results each time. Life usually doesn't work that way. If we want something to change, we have to change something ourselves.

So read through the book, identify what you think are your main problem areas and then determine your best course of action. Then make the changes you feel need to be made. Monitor the results and either stay on course or make corrections until you find the approach and solutions that work best for you.

Believe me when I tell you that you can do this. It is not that difficult and it sure isn't rocket science. Trust me when I tell you that you have the skills and abilities to change you behavior when you need to. This book will give you the information and then you implement it.

Sometimes the very first step is the hardest. But once you take that first step and see that it made something easier, better or less stressful, you discover the motivation to keep going and change something. Positive results provide a ton of encouragement and motivation.

But what if something doesn't work? Or what if something doesn't work like you expected? In those cases it might get a little frustrating. But don't let it get you down. Instead of thinking of it as a failure, think of it as one more thing you know doesn't work which will increase your odds of success now.

Last, but certainly not least, your chances for success are greatly increased if you have a plan and carefully think about what you are going to do before you actually do it. Granted sometimes you will act on intuition and judgment but when you have the opportunity to plan ahead and think things through, then by all means do so.

You will find almost all parts of this book easy to understand and read. We designed it to be that way. We don't use long words when short ones will do. We don't use a lot of technical jargon and fancy terminology. We wrote this book to make it easy to understand so everyone will have little or no problem understanding everything.

You can do this and we know it. Now is the time for you to start believing it as well.

What is a Difficult Person?

We all know difficult people. They are all around us and sometimes it seems that there are far too many of them. These are the people who make our lives more difficult or more stressful. They often stand in our way of getting things done or put roadblocks in front of us every chance they get. We see them at work, at school, in our neighborhood, at stores and even at church.

There are different types of difficult people. Here are just a few of the most common types. You might encounter a different type but most likely they will fall into one or more of the following types:

Liar

These are the people who cannot be trusted. They will lie, cheat and steal to get what they want or to advance whatever personal agenda they have at that moment. They might want to make themselves look better or make you look worse. It really doesn't matter which as they have the same net effect.

Liars are dangerous because you may believe something they said and make decisions or take actions based on those lies.

The results of those decisions will be on you and you might find yourself accepting blame for something done based on those lies.

Work Stealer

We have all encountered the co-worker who readily takes credit for things others have done. Whether it might be as blatant as putting their name on a report or project someone else has done or just taken credit by claiming another person's work as their own, the results are the same.

These people are difficult because you cannot readily confide in them or work with them because you know they will get the results of your efforts and claim them as their own before you can. This makes them look more valuable and more productive than others in the office.

Entitled

Personally I just cannot stand people who feel entitled to things just because they are available and others might have them. While we are entitled to some things in life, such as a safe place to live and not to feel threatened or discriminated against, these people take it to the extreme.

They feel they are entitled to a big home because their friend has one. It makes no difference that their friend went to medical school or worked hard and risked their entire savings to build a new company while they sat at home playing video games. No, they feel that everything should be handed to them without work or effort.

It appears that more and more people have become infected with the entitlement virus, as I like to say, because advertising and media tell them they should have this and that they can use credit to get that, all because they deserve it.

Entitled people rarely pull their own weight and expect others to help them or outright give them things without working for them. This places an added burden on the rest of us.

Ambitious

These are the people who are ruthless in getting what they want in life. While everyone should go after what they want in life, they should not do that at the expense of others or by hurting others.

Ambitious people might try to make you look bad so they will look better and get the promotion or increase in salary. They might even take steps to discredit you so that you will be one of the people let go in the upcoming layoffs and not them.

We have all heard the expression that he walked over people to get where he is today. Accomplishing a task or achieving a goal at the expense of others is not the right way to go and it causes pain and suffering in the lives of others.

Bully

A bully is the one of the worst types of difficult people. These are the people who take advantage of others through intimidation and physical force or violence. Bullies can be dangerous and cause physical and emotional harm to others.

Bullies tend to pick on weaker people who are not capable or likely to fight back or stand up to them. Bullies rarely target stronger people and usually will not act alone. A bully is far more likely to act in concert with others to make it an even more lopsided encounter.

Fear is the tool used most by bullies. They prey on people's weaknesses and rely on silence and fear to keep people in line so that they are not held accountable for their actions.

Know it All

These people are more annoying than difficult but they do make things harder for all of us. We all know someone who thinks they know everything about everything. They feel grossly superior and insist on everyone doing what they want because they know best.

These people often try and take control of every situation and project believing that only they know enough to get the proper results. They will discount anyone's opinions or thoughts feeling there are always superior or better.

Know it All's are usually more annoying than difficult but they still cam make life more difficult and stressful. This is compounded when they think they know everything but the reality is that they know little or nothing. As they say, a little knowledge can be dangerous in the wrong hands.

Aggressive

Aggressive people can be a handful because they will not stop at anything until they get what they want. Aggressive people can tend to be confrontational and will tend to try and steamroller over anyone that stands in their way.

Aggressive people can also be dangerous because they will often work behind the scenes either gathering support or sabotaging efforts in order to further their own causes or agenda. You might not become aware of certain things until it is too late.

Intimidating

Somewhat similar to bullies, intimidating people use certain tactics to get what they want or are looking for.

People might be intimidating because of their size, personality or just their habits. Sometimes people are seen as intimidating even though they make no attempt to intimidate anyone.

There are several types of intimidation. We have physical as well as emotional intimidation. People might use this intimidation to get you to back down, change your opinion, or provide or withhold support in certain situations.

Unstable

There are people in this world who are emotional or mentally unstable. These are the people who might not qualify as disabled or handicapped but still are not capable of restraint or normal and rational thought.

Some of these people can become quite dangerous at times and you should be careful and watch for signs of potential violence and serious behavior.

If you suspect someone might qualify as an unstable individual you should protect your personal safety at all times. Try never to be alone with such a person and take steps not to incite any negative emotions or behavior. If the term "walking on eggshells" had a place, this would be it.

Unstable people usually will exhibit some warning signs that dangerous behavior might be forth coming. Short tempers, emotional outbursts that are not in proportion to the situation are just a few warning signs.

If you know of such an individual, or if you have witnessed disturbing or warning signal behavior, tell your manager or other escalated party or department immediately. It might also be a good idea to distance yourself from this individual if possible until the situation s calmed down and well in hand.

Be Prepared & Anticipate

Sometimes it is very hard to figure out exactly what to do when we have to make a quick decision. What we think at the moment is the right thing to do may very well turn out to be wrong. That is because we don't take or have the time to think things through and understand the ramifications of the decisions we make.

It is always better to take some time to think things through before acting. Granted, there will be times when this is not going to be possible but most of the time we can take a minute or two to think about what is best. Even if it means taking an unneeded bathroom break or going out for a cup of coffee, take those few moments.

Most of the time we will know when we will be called upon to interact with a difficult person. We will know the difficult people from work or within family or with friends and neighbors. We will have time to prepare ourselves for what is to come and determine what we will do and how we will react.

It is always best to have a pro-active plan in place. If you know you are going to have to spend the day with "Mr. Ambitious" you can prepare yourself by understanding what is likely to take place and tell yourself that you only have to deal with him for 5 or 6 hours. You are far more likely to get through the experience unscathed with an advance plan.

We all have had instances where we do or say things we later regret. That is because we reacted on the spur of the moment because we were not prepared or because we had not given the situation proper thought. Words cannot be taken back or unsaid. The damage they cause will remain long after the apology has been given. So I'm sure we all can agree that it is best to think first and say things or take action later.

Keep in mind that this sort of thing is how most difficult people want it to be. They thrive on keeping you off balances and getting you to do or say things that will help them in furthering their own agenda or goals. They WANT you to feel flustered and they WANT you to act on impulse rather than in a controlled fashion

So don't let people control your environment or your responses. Take responsibility for your own actions and decisions and make them with carefully thought out responses. In other words, play on your playing field, not theirs.

But what do you do when things cannot wait and a situation pops up where you have to act immediately with little or no time to think in advance or plan?

These situations do come up and the only thing we can do is make the very best decision possible based on information we already have in our minds.

But the best thing we can always do under these circumstances is go back after the fact and see how the decisions were made and what the outcome was. If the outcome was what you hoped or expected, then congratulations! Your thought process was sound and the response appropriate.

But if things back fired or the decision was not the right one, go back and see why you made the wrong choice. What happened that caused the error? What were the circumstances and why did you make the choices you made? Understanding where something went wrong is a wonderful learning tool that can help us avoid repeating that mistake in the future.

Not everything works all the time on all people and in all situations. What might sound like a logical and sound choice now might fail miserably later and the reasons become evident. But we look into those failures to see what went wrong and we learn from it. Then, when similar situations show up later, we make different decisions and have different responses.

But it is always best to be aware and think before responding. Take a break, think things through and learn from your mistakes. If you can do this you will find that your skills in dealing with all kinds of people will dramatically improve over time. Experience is a wonderful teacher if we just pay attention to the lessons it provides.

It is Not Going to Go Away

As a rule of thumb, leaving a situation or problem alone will not make it go away. Instead, it is likely to get worse and require even more action and effort to resolve in the future. So if there is a difficult person in your life, it is best to figure out ways to deal with them now rather than later.

Letting someone continue to bother you or derail you from your goals and dreams is not an acceptable alternative. Some kinds of people will increase their efforts to disturb you if they see you are willing to put up with that kind of treatment. So ignoring it is not a viable option.

Make it a policy to at least identify the difficult people in your life as soon as possible. This will enable you to better become proactive and figure out the best way to deal with them. You decision might be to ignore them because their effect on you is minimal.

Sometimes people do things to people or treat them a particular way to see what kind of reaction they will get.

When their efforts are ignored, or when they get no reaction at all, they might give up and move on to someone else to see if that person will give them the reaction they want.

Do NOT confuse this with not doing anything. Not doing anything means allowing the situation to continue or escalate. That is something we should avoid. But, after careful thoughtful you decide the best way of dealing with a person is to ignore them, then that is your plan of action.

You might have seen the same behavior by someone else and noticed how effective it was in stopping the person dead in his or her tracks. So naturally you figure the same approach should work for you. So you figure that you should give it a try.

As a rule of thumb, however, most situations will only get worse over time if left unaddressed. The earlier you become engaged in the situation and take appropriate action, the better off you will be.

Stress

For those of you who wonder if it really is worth the time and effort to deal with a difficult person, let me tell you that these people can be responsible for huge amounts of stress in our lives. Stress is something that can be harmful to our health as well as change our outlook and the way we deal with things in our lives.

Stress is known to cause or at least contribute to several health related issues such as high blood pressure, heart disease, depression and many other things. Sometimes it causes no side effects but the damage is being done. At the very least, it removes some or much of the enjoyment from our daily activities.

Think of how you would feel about your job if you office were full of people who gave you a hard time. Think about how people who feel bullied by people often become so depressed that they go as far as taking their own lives to stop the pain. Though this is an extreme reaction, the stress in our lives needs to be controlled and minimized.

Difficult people cause stress by making things more difficult or less enjoyable.

They may inspire a reaction of fear like in the case of school yard bullies who frighten their victims and sometimes cause them to skip school.

As we get older we might find less enjoyment in work, withdraw from social activities, or even move to a new job or to a new town to avoid conflict and fear. This is why it is so important to address issues and people early so that we can all get the enjoyment out of life that we deserve.

While it is not possible to remove all stress from our lives, it is important to address the causes of stress and minimize their impact. Trying to mend relationships or minimize their impact on our lives is one very effective way of reducing stress.

It is important to realize that you usually have a choice when it comes to who you interact with and how that interaction is handled. You should not have to put up with abuse, bullying or negative behavior by anyone else. There are steps you can and should take and we will start going over these starting now.

Do not feel that this is not worth your time. Do not feel that you are somehow to blame for this type of treatment. Some people are just mean and abusive towards other people. This is a hard fact to accept but it is true. So when something happens to you, or when someone is negatively effecting your life, it is time to let them know that this is not OK with you and that you are going to fight to make your life better.

You owe it to yourself to protect your health and future longevity by creating the least stressful lifestyle you possibly can. So don't let anyone intimidate or force you to live a lifestyle you don't want to. Because living a lifestyle that is different from who you are carries with it an entirely different form of stress.

Stress you just don't need in life.

Abuse

Before we take the first step in showing you how to deal with difficult people and minimize the effect these people have on your life, we need to talk about the type of abuse these people can cause in your life.

Just so that we are 100% clear, an activity does not have to be physical to constitute abuse. In fact, sometimes emotional or mental abuse is far more damaging to a person than physical abuse. Bruise and broken bones will usually heal in days or weeks. But emotional scars can last for a lifetime.

People can be abusive in many ways. The can hit you or tell you over and over and over again how worthless you are. They can steal you work, take credit for your accomplishments or ridicule you in front of others. This is all abuse. Abuse does not have to put you in a hospital bed to be classified as abuse.

Let me be absolutely clear here. If there is someone in your life who is causing you grief and damaging your personality, your reputation or causing you to alter who and what you are, that is abuse. And you should not tolerate it.

If you are being abused, seek help and assistance from others. Sometimes it is just too big of a battle to be handled by one person. Sometimes we have to report the abuse or behavior to others. While our first attempts should always be to resolve things quietly and privately, there will be times when this will just not work.

Sometimes bullies only respond to similar behavior from other. So you might have to get outside help to confront the bully. Maybe you have to enlist the help of your manager to control office behavior that is abusive.

This is NOT being a tattle-tale or a "rat" or anything like that. What it really is is your way of standing up for yourself and what you believe is right in this world. It is being strong enough to say no to abusive behavior and standing up for your rights.

Now some of you might be thinking that this book is about difficult people and that we are blowing this up all out of proportion. In some cases you might be right but some people in this world do treat people horribly.

There are spouses in this world who torment their spouse, call them worthless and useless every single day. Can you stand there and tell me this is not abusive behavior and this is not a difficult person to deal with? Yes, the behavior is extreme. But the effects of even low level abuse can be devastating.

The first step in dealing with difficult and abusive people is finding the strength and courage to stand up for yourself.

In some cases you might need to find the courage to stand up for someone else as well. Seeing abusive behavior and turning away because it was not directed to you is not an acceptable reaction. It might not be smart to directly intercede, but you should make others aware of what's going on.

I look back at some things in my past where I had to deal with some unpleasant people and I have to say that I regret not standing up for myself or for others. I still have regrets and memories dating back 30-40 years about things I wish I had done differently.

The good thing is that society has changed remarkably over the last few decades and activity that used to be ignored and swept under the rug so to speak are now being talked about openly and people are encouraged not to tolerate it anymore.

I just want to make sure that everyone understands that they have a right to a peaceful existence on this earth. They should not be victimized by others and they should not be made to feel that this behavior is to be tolerated or accepted.

I am telling you that you have a right to stand up for yourself and a right to take measures to stop this sort of behavior. It is when people like you and I do nothing that bad and difficult people are allowed to continue and even escalate their behavior.

I have said it already and I will say it again. If we do nothing, nothing changes. So don't do nothing, do something. If not for you, do it for someone who might not be strong enough to do it for themselves.

Stay Calm & Rational

Regardless of the type of person you are dealing with, one of the universal keys to success in dealing with difficult people is to stay calm. Some people try certain tactics in order to upset people and get them angry. That is because several things happen when people get angry and this plays right into their objectives.

When people get angry, here are some of the things that happen:

We lose focus

When we get angry, very often common sense flies right out the window. We get distracted and we no longer think in a calm and straight forward manner. We start acting with emotion instead of facts. In other words, we quickly get carried away emotionally.

We fail to Communicate Effectively

Have you ever tried to carry on a conversation with a really made person? It is almost impossible to get any real and meaningful information from the conversation because it is all filled with raw emotion.

Things get exaggerated, fiction becomes fact and any rational thought has almost a zero chance of entering the conversation.

More than half of what we say lies not only in the words but in the emotion behind those words. When a person is angry or upset, emotions take control and there becomes little chance in getting any kind of negotiation started.

When people get angry it's like a wall is put up and they stand at that wall and they refuse to allow anything to get through. They will not bend or change their mind, they will not listen to opposing views or opinions, and anger will swiftly squash any attempt to get something positive resolved.

We lose judgment and perspective

Life is a series of negotiations. No one gets everything they want all of the time. It's a process of give and take that starts from the minute we are born. Most of us understand this. But angry people lose their perspective and really believe that any form of negotiation is an admission of defeat or failure.

Life is not a win-lose type of process. Everything in life should be a win-win where everyone gets at least some of what they want out of every situation. But when people get angry, they lose the perspective that others have needs as well. When this happens the win-win process goes away and "winner take all" is substituted. This makes the situation worsen instead of getting better.

We do not Act Rationally

Angry people tend to demand more often to the point where their demands are not only excessive but irrational. Anger gets us excited and excited people demand more and more. So trying to negotiate with an angry person is going to make resolution more difficult and more costly.

Anger and rational thought are 180 degrees apart. We need to get people calmed down to the point where rational thought is possible. Sometimes this can be done in minutes, other times it might take hours or even days. But you cannot expect an angry person to act or think rationally.

We do Things we Regret

Who reading this book has never said something in anger that they later came to regret? Who has used offensive and hurtful words in anger or insulted someone or hurt their feeling during an angry outburst.

We all have done whether we care to admit it or not. But anger has ruined many a relationship, caused countless people to lose their jobs and may other bad events to happen.

It is most often far better to bite your tongue and walk away before you say or do something you will later come to regret. The filter we have between our mouth and our brain lets almost everything through when we are angry. As we have said before, you can apologize for the words that were said but you can never take them back.

Situations Escalate Far More Rapidly

Two calm people talking can usually resolve almost any legitimate situation. But when one or both of those people are angry, the situation can go from calm to physical violence in seconds.

I like to think about anger as being a straight line where on the left side is calm and on the far right is physical violence. If you are angry you might start in the middle of that line or a little to the right and physical violence, or similar activity, lie just a short distance away. That is not a good thing. We want to start out on the left side near the calm point on the line. That way there is movement allowed before things get out of hand.

Everything we do and say should be focused on moving everyone toward the left (or calm) side and we should avoid doing or saying anything that will bring people further to the right side.

Personally, I always try to remain calm even though I might be angry on the inside. The main reason for this is that I want to remain in control of my emotions and my own thought process. I want to hear what is being said, watch what is being done, and be able to see things as they really are, not something colored or influenced by anger or emotion.

Another reason to remain calm is that sometimes when we are angry we take something innocent and unintentional and blow it all out of proportion.

The saying is that someone made a mountain out of a molehill. But when we are angry, we often do that.

How many times in your relationship with a friend or spouse were you angry and then some little thing happened and World War 3 was created by your reaction to it? Talk about moving someone over the extreme right almost immediately!

Calm people are far more apt to remain in control over their emotions and are able to control what they say and do so as to not inflame the situation even more. They are also better able to document things accurately and make sound judgments as to what needs to happen next.

Calm people are far more likely to exit the situation with their reputation and dignity intact. When we act in a controlled and rational manner people see that and learn to respect us for that ability. But when we go ballistic and rant and rave and act undignified or unprofessional, that makes us look bad.

Sometimes this is exactly why people do certain things to us. They want to goad us into doing or saying something that reflects poorly on us and then act all innocents and say how sorry they feel for you. All the while laughing on the inside at what they were able to do.

Remember when we talked about some people doing things to make you look bad so they in turn look better? Playing into this by allowing yourself to lose control is exactly what they are looking for.

So the next time you have to interact with a difficult person, someone who manages to push all your buttons, prepare yourself and make a strong effort to stay calm and in control. Remove yourself from the situation if you feel you are starting to lose control. There are several ways to do this.

Take a bathroom break; tell the other person you have an appointment. If the encounter is over the phone tell them you have another call, or maybe a scheduled conference call, and that you will call them back later.

Then when you have calmed back down and have had a chance to think about how you should react and what you should do, you can resume the encounter usually with much better results.

Another benefit of taking this approach is that many times the other party will have calmed down a bit as well by the time you resume discussions. With both people more calm, you stand a much better chance of resolving the situation in a more positive manner.

Do Not Take Things Personally

Many times we take everything far too seriously. A comment made in jest might be taken seriously or we might read more into something than really exists. Most of the time we do this is when we already have negative feelings toward the person that said it.

We have all had friends who have made fun of us in jest and those comments are laughed off because they were made in fun. Even when a friend crosses the line with a comment or act, we usually tell them to knock it off but don't really get too upset.

But when someone we perceive as difficult or negative should say the same thing, we read into the comment content that may not be there. It might be that person's way of trying to fit in or join in the fun. Or it might really be a negative comment. Sometimes you just never can know for certain.

It is important to understand and accept that every comment that is made to you is not a personal affront or attack.

Some people are extremely sensitive and you cannot really say anything to them without seemingly offending them. If that is you, I have a bit of advice for you.

Get over it. Stop taking life and yourself too seriously.

People who take everything seriously are not all that much fun to hang out with. It is always important to remember that the way we act with others has a dramatic influence on the way they act with us. If we are fun loving and positive, people will want to be around us because they will have a great time and a lot of laughs.

But if we are too serious and take exception to everything that is said, or if we constantly challenge the comments of others then we no longer are all that much fun to deal with. When this happens we ourselves might even be considered difficult by others. That is the last thing we want in our lives.

When we take things personally, they are no longer words or acts, but personal attacks. We might respond more with emotion than with common sense. In other words, when we take things personally, our rational thought process takes a hit and we might say or do something we will later regret.

When we take something personally we also increase our stress level which is not good either. Being able to detach ourselves from the situation and remain objective is very difficult when we take things personally. So here's one more piece of advice:

So cut yourself and others some slack in life. Let some comments roll off your back. Have a laugh at your own expense from time to time. Relax just a little bit. It's important to enjoy life and not make every comment or act a personal affront or attack.

Picking Your Battles

There are big problems and there are minor issues in life. There are those comments and actions that make a huge impact and then there are those that barely effect us and are a very small part of the big picture. We shouldn't treat everything the same. We need to make an appropriate response based on the situation. And sometimes the best response is no response at all.

Parents usually understand this. They might let little things slide in order to raise their kids in a positive atmosphere where their kids feel safe and loved while not being badgered to death. If their parent were to pick on them or discipline them for every little thing, they would become afraid to come to them with problems or advice.

Stress is another reason that we might want to consider being a little less strict and exercise a little more acceptance towards other people and the things they do. You would find yourself letting some things go and along with that would go the stress associated with that particular situation.

For example, if a co-worker has an annoying habit, maybe he slurps his coffee or stretches his 15 minute coffee break to 20 minutes, you can either get in his face or report him or just let it go. After all, chances are someone else is aware of it also and you should be not appointing yourself the office police force. It's a little thing, the impact is relatively small, and the negatives that are possible if you confront him about it are too many.

But if that same person is stealing from people's desk or stealing supplies or bullying people that is something on an entirely different level with much more severe impact or consequences. That is usually a battle you need or should become part of.

What we are saying is to pick your battles carefully. Let some small stuff slide so you can tackle the big issues that may come up later. You don't want to get the reputation as a complainer because you pick on people for everything they do every day. If you get that reputation then when the big stuff comes along no one will listen to you. They will think it is just one more thing you are complaining about.

Some people will actually encourage you to complain because they know once you get that reputation then no one will listen to you and they can continue to get away with the things you know about. Difficult people are sometimes more difficult to deal with because they attack you from so many different sides you don't often see what's coming!

So the next time something little comes along where the impact is small and the consequences are minimal, think twice when it comes to taking action. Don't be afraid of the so-called "slippery slope" where things rapidly go downhill once little things are allowed to go unchallenged. Though that theoretically might be possible, it is usually not the case.

Do not Retaliate:
Be the Bigger Person

Sometimes our first reaction when someone does something to us is to retaliate. To let them know that we are not going to tolerate that kind of action or behavior. But it is important to understand that there are ways or letting people know you will not tolerate something than to response in similar fashion.

You know the story because you have witnessed it many times in your life. Person A does something to Person B and then B responds with something a little bigger or worse against A. Then A responds with something worse to B who responds to A and so on and so on.

Though sometimes this is all done in good fun, when people do things against each other and the other person retaliates, things can quickly get out of hand. The events get worse and worse or more dangerous over time and the end result is always something much more than either party expected.

Retaliation is a juvenile way of dealing with problems. In the eyes of the law you are not justified in harming or damaging the property of someone else because he did the same to you. "An eye for an eye" might have worked back in Biblical times but it is not accepted behavior today.

At times retaliation is thought by some of us to be a way to get the offensive behavior to stop. The thought is that if you do something bad to someone else, they will be afraid to do something again to you because of the repercussions. Logically this appears to make sense but reality often takes a different response.

Reality says if you do something to another person, that person will be so angry they will adopt an "I'll show them" mentality and devise something larger or worse as a response. One would think this would be a primarily a youthful or child's response but unfortunately this line of thinking travels all the way into adulthood. The only difference is that adults have more resources at their disposal.

Retaliation is a form of escalation as the acts get bigger and bigger over time. This causes the situation behind these acts to worsen as well. Hard feelings, anger and frustration build over time and this is not good as far a resolving the original problem is concerned.

I am not telling you to sit by and do nothing or ignore things that happen to you. I am not even saying you should laugh them off when they do hurt either

. But we should avoid retaliation at all costs. Rarely does anything good come from it.

Instead of retaliation, consider talking with the offending party and letting them know you do not appreciate that kind of behavior or activity and ask them to stop. While they may look at you like you were crazy, you have at least notified them and made a request for them to stop.

After that if they don't stop, you can report them to your boss or to the authorities and put it on record that this has happened before and that you informed them to stop. They cannot plead ignorance because you have told them.

If someone is doing something at work that makes you time in the workplace unpleasant, ask them politely to stop. Office pranks, while enjoyed by some, are not a given right in the workplace. Any objectionable or unlawful behavior that is not welcomed by another person should be eliminated in the workplace.

In another chapter we mentioned that some people do things with the intent on getting you mad or angry. This plays into their overall agenda of making you look foolish or bad in the eyes of others. Well, those same people might do things to you with the intent of getting you to retaliate.

Then, once you do retaliate they play the role of the victim and act hurt or wounded. "Can you believe what Stan did to me yesterday? It was totally uncalled for and very mean. The man is a bully." They might say.

They fail to mention the 12 things they did to you to illicit your retaliation but the fact remains that you actually did do what he said you did and now everyone knows it. So your reputation is damaged and they wind up looking like the poor victim.

Some people do things to others just for personal fun. For some perverse reason they enjoy inflicting pain or hurt on other people. When it comes to dealing with those people, you have to be firm and let them know that you do not appreciate the behavior and that you will not tolerate it again in the future. Let them know you will document it and report it to either management or the authorities whichever is appropriate.

Then, if they continue their behavior follow through with your threat of reporting them. Now don't report people for little stupid things or you will just get laughed out of human resources. "He took a paper clip after I told him to get his own box of paper clips" is not a reportable human resource issue.

But "He put soap in my sandwich this morning and he has done so in the past and I told him to stop" might be something you might want to report. Whatever you do don't mess with his lunch because if he reports you it could cost you your job! Life isn't always fair and the good are often punished for the acts of the bad.

So the next time someone does something to you, tell them to stop. Document what occurred and let them know future acts will not be ignored and they will be reported.

Then follow through with your actions if the same thing happens again.

Keep in mind that this type of behavior is rarely against just one person. Chances are that others have incurred the same behavior or acts by the same individual. One person's complaints may not be acted upon especially if no proof is available. These people are clever and sometimes leave no proof that it was them who actually did it. But if several people file complaints a pattern arises that makes the case easier to proof and support.

Our efforts should not be on retaliation but on stopping the behavior I the future. We should be doing things to escalate the behavior, we should do doing things to control or stop it all together.

So keep your wits together, keep calm and do not retaliate. Follow the steps outlined her to stop this behavior or have the person disciplined and held accountable for it.

NOTE:

If someone does something that physically harms you or another individual, or does something that places you or another person's safety at risk, take immediate steps to report it. Giving someone a second chance to do this type of activity could have fatal results!

Talk It Over

Before we get into specifics and other techniques targeted towards dealing with difficult people, we really need to discuss one very easy, yet sometimes extremely effective, technique for resolving conflict and disagreements.

It is amazing how many disputes or situations get out of hand because people just refuse to sit down and talk things over. Maybe there are personality clashes involved or maybe people actually do dislike each other. But just sitting down with someone and talking things over can sometimes make things a lot better.

It might seem like a very basic and common sense approach but communications are just not strong points for some people. They are either afraid to show their emotions or even show what they feel is weakness in front of others.

In some cases it is a case of who has the bigger ego and who is willing to make the first move. Sometimes two people both insist that the other person be the one to come to them to initiate things. They insist on this so that they appear to be the stronger party or the supposed winner.

The problem is that the longer something goes on, the more difficult it becomes to stop and resolve. What might have been handled with a simple conversation a week or month ago might now require the intervention of a manager or a third party to get things settled. Sometimes entire relationships are destroyed because the two people refused to talk about simple things.

Difficult people are usually difficult to talk to as well. They sometimes have their own reasons or agenda for doing what they do and they are usually not willing to share that with anyone. After all, if someone's plan is to discredit you in order to get that job promotion that is coming up they surely are not going to admit that to you.

But sometimes things are misinterpreted or it's just an honest mistake that causes the problem. Maybe the person has good intentions but failed to realize how their actions or attitude would be interpreted. In those cases all it might take is a little conversation to explain your thoughts and feeling and things can go along much better from that point forward.

There have been times when I did something with all the best intentions but someone took offense for reasons that I did not take into consideration. Once I was made aware of that I saw how things could have been handled differently and I changed my approach. All it took was being made aware that I was doing something that was not being accepted very well.

So before we get all analytical and try and come up with all kinds of plans and actions steps and all of that, why not at least make an attempt to talk things over with the other person. That might be all that needs to happen. You have very little to lose and a heck of a lot to gain.

Offer to Help

I ask you to bear with me for a bit in this chapter because what I will be asking you to consider might be totally opposite to what you really think you should do. But sometimes this form of action can have very positive results when used in the right situations.

Have you heard the expression "You can catch more flies with honey than you can with vinegar"? That means you can accomplish more with positive or kind action than you can by being mean or confrontational.

That means if you have someone who is very difficult to get along with or interact with, there might be a reason why that person is that way. Maybe they were the victim of unfair events earlier in life. Maybe they were abused or taken advantage of. Maybe they were treated poorly at a previous job and now are suspicious of everyone.

Whatever the reason might be, you might have to work or be around this person for quite some time so it makes sense to try and "win them over" or move the relationship to a more positive level.

You can often accomplish this by acting nicer to the person or offering to help them with a particular task or project. By showing yourself to be more of an ally than an enemy, you might just start getting a more positive response from them as well.

Years ago I took a job in an office equipment dealer and one of the first things I was told is that one of the tech, an older gentleman, was ornery and very difficult to get along with. "Just stay away from him." Was the advice I was given.

Well, I had some conversations with him over a few days and I commented on the quality of his work. I didn't go overboard but I told him that I appreciated the fact that he worked hard and repaired things very well and that he had the lowest return rate of everyone. I did that for a period of a couple of weeks.

One day at a meeting I mentioned that I needed someone to make a trip the next morning and it needs to happen very early in the morning at the client's request. It was a trip no one wanted to make and I was hoping someone would volunteer so I didn't have to ask someone to do it.

To everyone's surprise. The supposed ornery old man said "I'll go." Everyone's jaw dropped. When I thanked him after the meeting, he said "Hey, you're always very nice to me so it's only right I treat you the same way." He didn't say another word and neither did I. But from that day on he would do anything I asked of him and more.

That is not to say that this will work for everyone. Some people will be difficult just because it is their nature. You can try all you want and all you will get is a slap in the face for your efforts. For those people, give it a try and when it doesn't work, well no one can say you didn't try.

But every time you can turn a difficult person into a friend or an ally, you make both of your lives just that much better. We are all the products of our previous life experiences. What happened in the past has helped create who we are today. That doesn't mean those things are etched in stone.

All it might take is one person treating that person with dignity and respect to get the ball rolling in the other direction. It is well worth the effort as the benefits far outweigh the risks.

Dignity & Respect

This is going to be a short chapter but also a very important one. It's one of those topics that should be considered common sense but for some reason it is lost in a lot of people today. That topic is the need to treat everyone with dignity and respect.

If you take a lot of difficult people and look at how they treat people, odds are they don't treat people very well. They can be rude, obnoxious, condescending or even abusive. The problem with that kind of treatment is that it really does not inspire anyone to treat them any better. After all, you would go to the wall for a good friend when they needed help but that obnoxious guy who belittles you at the office? Well, he just gets what he deserves.

I take a somewhat controversial attitude into life. That attitude is that everyone should be treated with dignity and respect. I believe everyone has the right to expect that they will be treated with dignity and respect from everyone else. Unfortunately, that is not always the case.

Now that attitude itself might not be controversial but I take it one step further and say that everyone should be treated with dignity and respect even though they might not treat others the same way.

Look, it is easy to be nice to someone who is nice to you. But it sometimes can be really difficult to be nice to someone who just screwed you over at work or at home. That is where the concept really gets put to the test.

As we said in a previous chapter, there will always be difficult people who will remain difficult no matter what we do. But that doesn't mean we have the right to treat them poorly as well. There will be a group, however, that will respond to you differently when you treat them right.

Think about how hard it is to treat someone poorly who treats you very well. Can you ridicule or make life difficult for someone who always treats you well and who helps you out when you need it? You might never become close friends but you are likely to be able to get along if you just give it a chance.

A major part of interpersonal skills dictates that how we treat others also has a profound impact on how those people treat us. Even if we treat people nicer from a purely selfish point of view because we want something from them, treating people better will still produce better results.

In life we do things a certain way because we believe that "works" for us in our lives. We might treat one way because that keeps us from getting hurt.

Or, we might treat people a certain way because that was the way we were brought up to treat them. Regardless, we need to wake up and take measure of how we treat certain people in our lives.

Let's start right here and now making a concerted effort to treat everyone, and I mean everyone, better in our lives. Let's make a strong effort to treat everyone with dignity and respect no matter how they treat us.

This is not about letting others take advantage of us. It is all about being the bigger person and taking initiative in trying to make things better in our lives.

This isn't going to work on everyone. I readily admit that. But the great thing is that it doesn't have to work on everyone to make a huge difference in this world. If we can make a difference in one person's life then our efforts are well placed.

This isn't about demanding perfection; it is about making a small difference. The thing about small differences is that they start adding up to create big differences. After a while something small can transform into something truly life changing.

This book is not about performing miracles or changing the world. It is about learning how to deal effectively with difficult people. We can accomplish that to a great extent by committing ourselves to treating everyone, good or bad, with dignity and respect.

The added bonus of going through life this way is that others will look at you more favorably and treat you better as well. So if for no other reason than a purely selfish one, let's all start treating everyone else with dignity and respect.

Not starting tomorrow, starting right now.

Communicating
Effectively

I truly believe many of today's problems are
caused by poor communication. By
misunderstanding what other people are
saying, we either waste time and resources or
we do the wrong things. Either way, this can
cause major problems in our lives and our
relationships.

Sometimes the most difficult people are the
ones you cannot "read". The people who are
difficult to understand and the people that you
never seem to know what they are looking for.
When you encounter such a person, it is likely
that they, or both of you, have a problem
communicating.

I mentioned the problem might be with
both of you because it is important to
understand that good communication between
two people is the responsibility of BOTH
people. Each person has the obligation and
responsibility to both listen and speak
effectively.

If either person does not hear properly or voice their needs effectively, the entire process breaks down, and misunderstanding takes place.

Though entire books have been written about the communication process, we will give you the basics right her so you can get started communicating better and more effectively.

Listening

Contrary to popular belief, LISTENING is the most important part of the communication process. It is not the words we use or how we talk even though those are also important. No, listening is the most important part of the communication process.

Think about it for a minute. If you don't really hear what the other person is saying, how can you choose the correct words and the correct response? How can you possibly carry on an informed and mutually beneficial conversation with another person?

Let's say you were having a conversation with a very nice co-worker. He was trying to get your input on an important project but the conversation went something like this:

Co-worker: Bill, I need some input on the quarterly financial report. Can you give me a hand with this?

You: My project is due Tuesday

Co-worker: I know your project is due Tuesday but can you give me an hour this afternoon just to get me started?

You: I should have it all wrapped up by Monday afternoon.

Co-worker: So you can't help me this afternoon?

You: this project was really a bear.

Co-worker: Forget it. I'll ask Bill.

Now that conversation was probably very frustrating for your co-worker because it didn't appear that you were concentrating or listening at all to what he was saying. You never answered his questions. Instead you made statements that were unclear as far as the context of the question. To your –co-worker, you might appear to be one of those difficult people we are talking about even though that might not be the case!

Here is how the conversation should have gone:

Co-worker: Bill, I need some help on the quarterly financial report. Can you give me a hand with this?

You: sure. But I have a report due Tuesday.

C0-worker: I know you r report is due Tuesday but maybe you could give me an hour this afternoon to get me started.

You: I planned to have my report done by Monday so I guess I can give you an hour this afternoon. Does 3 o'clock work for you?

Co-worker: 3 o'clock in fine. I'll come to your office. Thanks for the help. I didn't feel like asking Bill. You know more about this than he ever will.

See the difference in tone and results from the two conversations.

The first conversation left your co-worker frustrated and thinking you were difficult and frustrating to deal with. He was willing to go to a less qualified person just to get away from dealing with you.

But the second conversation went very well and he left feeling good about you and where this situation was heading. Both conversations took the same amount of time. But when you listened and made the appropriate responses, everything went much better.

Listening is critical to good communications. If you misinterpret something it might not make a difference how good a job you can do. If you produce the world's best report on the sales of women's shoes but your boss asked on a financial report on the cost of making women's shoes, your boss isn't going to be happy.

People get angry and frustrated when communications do not go easily, accurately and smoothly. Those frustrations turn into anger and then everything goes rapidly downhill.

Always listen to what the other person is saying. Never interrupt them or cut them off. Letting them talk allows them to vent their anger and frustrations and allows them to calm down. This will make the next communication go even easier. Plus, the extra words and information given by the person can help you make more accurate and informed decisions.

So, look, just shut up and listen, OK?

Separate Emotions from the Words

When we verbally communicate, we use both words and emotions. You can hear emotions behind the words. When you talk to someone over the phone, you can hear the anger and frustration in their voice. They might speak louder or more forceful. They might speak more rapidly or in a more excited voice. You can not only hear the words, you can hear the frustration and anger behind them.

When talking face to face, you can see the facial expressions and also view the body language as well. You can more easily see and experience how the other person fells but listening and seeing.

The most important thing to understand about anger and frustration is that they are huge roadblocks in the communications process. You cannot get very much accurate information from someone who is yelling and screaming at you.

You need to try and calm people down so the information they give you is more accurate and factual. If you cannot accomplish that right now then you need to find a way of postponing the conversation until everyone has calmed down. That is the only way to get accurate communication started.

The good part of being about to listen and hear anger and frustration is that you can get an idea of the severity of the problems and situation without actually asking about it or discussing it. If you hear anger and frustration in someone's voice then you know you better damned well take this issue seriously.

You know urgency is important and you know not to trivialize or minimize the problem with the other person.

Choose Words Carefully

Difficult people often look for any excuse to escalate things r introduce more problems into the situation. Because of this we need to choose our words and comments carefully, especially when the other party is already angry or frustrated.

We want to instill the feeling that you really want to help resolve the problem or help with the task. This means we should concentrate on using positive words and avoid negative words.

That means using words like can and will and avoid the use of worlds like can't, shouldn't and won't. As a rule people don't care what you can't or won't do. They want to hear what you can and will do. So always make an effort to make positive statements rather than negative ones.

Always remember that positive statements make people happier and more calm while negative statements make people angrier and more frustrated. Keep in mind that happier is always better as far as the communication process is concerned.

Smashing Down the Walls

The other interesting thing about people is that they rapidly erect "walls" between them and others when they hear something they don't think they want to hear.

If you tell someone a negative thing followed by two positive things, they often will only hear or remember the negative thing. Their ears and brain shut right down after the negative thing.

For example, let's say a customer wants you to match a price on a similar item available at another store. But the problem is the item is a better item than the one at the other store and you cannot match the price. If you tell him you can't match the price, they will shut down and not hear anything else you say. But if you say something like this, you might have a better shot:

"Our item is a better model and we include a free extra year warranty as well as free deliver to all our customers. When you factor those into the price at the other store, our price actually comes out cheaper."

That entire statement is positive and nowhere in that statement did you say that you cannot match the price. You gave all the benefits and inferred that no price match would occur but you did it all in a positive manner.

Difficult people want what they want and they expect, even demand, that you give it to them or there will be hell to pay. But during the communication process, if you keep things positive and tell them all you can give them, you will have a much higher chance of success.

Communications is critical to interacting with all kind of people. But difficult or demanding people make it even more critical. The more difficult or demanding a person is, the less tolerant they will be towards any mistakes or errors. Very often you won't get a second chance.

You must make sure you have the correct information and confirm that what you heard is what they meant. Because even if the error is theirs, you can be left holding the ball and taking the blame for the mistake.

Which brings us to another important part of the communication process:

Ask a LOT of Questions!

As we just mentioned, when dealing with difficult people, there usually is much less margin for error or mistakes. Since mistakes will just make things worse, we want to make every effort to make sure we have total understanding when it comes to what was just said or asked of us. This will help avoid future conflict and aggravation.

The best way to avoid confusion is to confirm information. The best way to confirm information is to ask a lot of questions. If there is something you are not sure of, ask a question so it becomes clear. If something was just a little too ambiguous, ask questions to clarify it so you make sure you are doing what you were asked.

Sometimes the most difficult person is the person who does not him or herself clear so they can escape blame should things not proceed well. These people leave certain decisions up to others so if their bosses don't like something they can turn around and say it was someone else's fault. I have worked for a few of those people in my day.

To further avoid confusion, do a summary of things after the conversation of topic has been concluded. Saying something along these lines can be helpful in confirming what was said without being obvious:

"Ok. Let's make sure we are all on the same page her. We decided on a purple cover with black lettering. The report is to be double sided with black and white graphs to keep costs down. It is to be completed by Friday and 50 copies are to be made for distribution on Monday."

Now if your boss goes to a meeting and someone complains about the graphs being in black and white they cannot blame you. If the report is done on Friday but the meeting was on Thursday, they can't blame you either! Well, I guess they can but you had the approval of everyone in the meeting so there will be witnesses.

Asking questions is not just for covering you butt as far as responsibility is concerned.

The more questions you ask the information you get. The more information get the more accurate your decisions will be. That means fewer wasted hours and fewer wasted resources. It also means you have a more detailed directive on what you are supposed to do so the final product will be more accurate and appropriate

The same goes for dealing with people. If someone asks you to do something but is not specific, ask for more specific instructions or more details.

Get them to commit on things that need to be committed on to make sure the outcome is what everyone thinks it will be.

Informed decisions are always better than assuming things. Planning a course of action based on clearly outlined information and fact is a lot better than making things up as you go. Whenever you are working on anything that involves other people, it is always worth the time and effort to get as much information as possible.

This will insure a more accurate and uniform product or result for everyone.

Consider Other Viewpoints

Every situation has two sides or viewpoints. Very often we might disagree with someone as to the direction or focus of a project or idea. Sometimes we might have different thoughts on how something should be handled or resolved. Life is not a one sided process and we should not go through life as if it was.

It is a very good and effective process to place yourself in the shoes of the other people when considering how something should be handled. If you are in an argument, take a moment to understand why the other person might feel the way they do. Sometimes this kind of insight can help dramatically in resolving things quickly and positively.

If you are in an argument or disagreement with other people, try and understand why they feel the way they do. There must be reasons for their feelings or they wouldn't have those feelings in the first place. It doesn't matter if you agree with their feeling or not. That is not the point. You don't have to agree but you do have to acknowledge them.

Ask people to explain their side and as they do listen to what they are saying. Have an open mind. Sometimes they might bring up valid points that you had not thought of. Sometimes they might think of things slightly differently and that might help as well. You might find yourself changing your position somewhat or you might not. But at least you will know why they feel the way they do.

Since much of life is a negotiation, it is important to understand the other people's viewpoints because this allows you to negotiate with everyone else so that everyone gets at least something they want or need from the resolution. We have said this before and I know we will say it again.

If you want to have the most success
dealing with other people
Try and give them as much of what they want
as possible.

Do not enter in relationships or situations believing that your views and opinions are the only ones that matter. If you fail to at least consider the views and opinions of others you will encounter far more difficult situations throughout your life.

Getting Input from Others

If you have difficult people in your life and you find that dealing with them is a difficult and stressful process, perhaps it's time to enlist the help of others. Sometimes getting the views and opinions of others can help you create a better or at least more effective plan of action.

Difficult people are difficult because what seems to work well with most people does not appear to work well with them. That does not mean you are right and they are wrong or vice versa. What it does mean is that you are probably going to have to change the way you deal with these people if you are going to have any kind of success at all.

People are all different. Therefore one approach will not work for everyone. What works well for you may wind up as a complete failure for me. The things you do at work might not translate well at home as well.

But the fact that people are different is something that we can use to our advantage.

It is something we can to help us resolve difficult or sensitive situations. Having others that we can turn to for their views or advice can be downright priceless. Perhaps these people have had similar situations in the past possibly even with the same person. Knowing what worked or didn't work for them can be a huge advantage when determining how you will proceed.

There are a lot of books and course from which we can learn a whole lot of information. But for some topics or skills, you cannot best personal experience. No book or seminar can be as effective as personally going though something or listening to someone else who has gone through the same thing.

Trial and error can work but you can also lose a lot of time and waste a lot of resources in the process. Having someone else tell you what they did with that person or in the same situation can make things a lot easier and faster for you. After all, why not learn from someone else's mistakes rather than make the same mistakes yourself?

Since we all have grown up with our own unique set of experiences and views, it just makes sense that someone else might be able to look at the same situation and see it as something totally different. By talking things through with that person you might wind up with either a new view on the matter or a new level of understanding.

Life is not designed to be gone through all alone.

We are social creatures and everyone needs the contact and interaction with other people. It is through that interaction that we learn new things, create new behaviors and grow as people.

Make an attempt to create a support structure in your life. Create something you can go to for advice, compassion and support. We can all agree that we are not going to come out on top in every situation. But we can all agree that life is much better when we have people we can turn to and share it with.

Give People More!

This chapter is so darned simple it's just amusing. The concept of giving people more is universal in its effectiveness and its ability to produce amazing results.

We are all people who want certain things out of life. When we get them we are happy and cooperative. When those things are denied we become angry and frustrated. When we get what we want, we become social. When we don't get what we want, we withdraw. Though this is overly simplified, the premise is clear.

> If we can give people the things in
> life they want,
> they will be easier and more
> co-operative to deal with.

I am not saying we should do everything for everyone and give everyone what they want. That is not reasonable or responsible. But the fact remains that people are more responsive when they feel they are getting something of benefit out of a situation.

Think about the times when you were taken advantage of in a situation.

When someone else got all they were asking for while you wound up with nothing. How did that make you feel? How did that influence the way you thought of that person the next time you interacted with them?

The day of the day-lose dynamic has passed. Today people insist on being treated fairly and equitably. They do not tolerate being taken advantage of as easily as they used to be. There was a time when people expected to be taken advantage of in certain situations. Those times today are few and far between.

This book is all about results and long term benefits. While many of the things you do will also bring you fast results, they are designed to provide those results for the long term as well. The same goes for dealing with difficult people.

If you take a person that is difficult to deal with for some reason and make an attempt to give them more of what they are looking for, you might see a change in their relationship with you. This is not some new-age, feel good, happy-happy nonsense. It appeals to basic human intelligence and emotion.

If someone gives you more of what you are looking for, you will feel more positive towards that person. That is just common sense. So if someone knows that you are a fair and reasonable person who also has their best interests at heart as well as your own, more people will co-operate with you.

As with most people, I have several resources I can use when I need to purchase something or get some help or assistance.

I always go where I feel I can get the best treatment and the best results. The same goes when people are concerned

I used to work as a Service Manager and I had several people who could do excellent work for me. But I used a core group of people the most. Why? Because those people gave me the best overall value. They treated people well, they did excellent quality work, and they responded quickly to my requests. In other words, in terms of total value, they gave me more.

In return, I supported them at a higher level and had their back when it came to rates and new opportunities. I made sure their business was taken care of in slow times and I had their back whenever the rare dispute came around. It was a mutually beneficial relationship. I should point out that I paid them at a higher level as well.

We should always look to give people more of what they need in any given situation. That might mean filling in for someone while they were on vacation even if we don't particular like them. It might mean partnering up with a difficult person on a project and holding their hand while working through a difficult task. In other words, it means showing these people that there is a benefit to being nicer to you.

This is no different than being nice to a friend or spouse. These people were initially attracted to you because something in your personality struck a chord with them.

We always will get better results and better treatment from others when we make an honest attempt to give them more as well.

The best way to approach any situation or negotiation is to ask yourself how you can give the other person more of what they need while still preserving your own interests. No one is asking you to sacrifice your best interests for someone else although sometimes that might be the smart thing to do.

Instead, we want to find ways for everyone to come out a winner in their eyes. While it might be better for you and your company to come up with a resolution that costs a little bit less, that resolution might alienate another person and cost you long term business.

It is important to understand that relationships have value. Even relationships with difficult people have value. In order to make the best decisions, you must understand the value of those relationships. This way you can make informed decisions based on both present and future values.

Don't be short sighted and make deals or handled interactions based only on what you will get today. Always think of the future and the benefits you might get a month or a year from now by giving something to somebody later.

We've said it once and we will say it again. Life and relationships are all about give and take.

Use the negotiation process to get what you need while also making sure the other person walks away with something they need as well. The relationships we have in business and at home deserve nothing less from you.

Align Yourself

Sometimes difficult people are thought of as difficult is because they work behind the scenes to get what they want often at your expense. They leave no evidence of their behavior behind and there is often nothing to indicate to anyone else that they were the cause of the problem or responsible for the outcome.

In other situations it may be just your word and against them. You know they were responsible but just cannot prove it. This is usually exactly what they are looking for. They want to cause trouble for you and they want you to know they were responsible but not be able to take any action against them.

This can be very frustrated because you are in a situation where damage, harm or stress is being introduced in your life but it appears you are powerless to do anything about it. But there is one very important thing you can and should do to protect yourself against difficult people. Align yourself with others.

There are many times in life where judgments are made not necessarily based on facts, but rather on the reputation and demeanor of the people involved. While judgments based on perception instead of reality are not often fair, they do exist and are very common.

If the difficult people you are trying to deal with are at work, you need to develop a support system. Your support system is comprised of people who know you and like you and believe in you. This does not happen overnight. It takes time and a lot of interaction before people really understand and believe in you. But it is worth the effort.

What we want is a group of people who believe in you to the extent that they will come to your defense whenever you are blamed for something or something is done or said that reflects poorly on you. Then it is not only your word against the other person but your word and the support of several other people that might tip the scales in your favor.

The same thing is needed in your personal life as well. Having a group of loyal friends that will show support and speak up for you when you need it is critical in today's society. There are a lot of opportunities in most people's personal lives that can expose them to a lot of difficult people and difficult behaviors.

In both cases, work and personal, our goal is to have a group of people who will speak up on your behalf whenever you are accused of any wrong doing or negative behavior.

You want several people who will step up and say "Look, I know John and we have worked together for a long time. There is absolutely no way he could have done this. Someone else just had to be behind this. I'm sure of it."

This is very important for the reason we just gave but also for one more reason that might even be more important: Some of those difficult people who do those things against you plot them out carefully and also develop their own support network to say the same things about them to deflect blame.

The guy trying to lie and cheat his way to that promotion you both want can be nice to people and gain their confidence all day long while laying the groundwork for having you take the blame for something he caused. So if you are the lone wolf in the office, or if you don't have people to come to your defense in the neighborhood or within your family, you are vulnerable.

This is a good pro-active defense strategy as well. Put yourself in the other person's shoes. If you wanted to make yourself look better by making someone else look bad, who would you choose as your target? The person well liked with the support and admiration of everyone in the office or the guy who keeps to himself and appears distanced from everyone else? If you have an active cell in your brain you would stay away from the popular and well supported person and attack the weaker opponent.

We have made a lot of reference that make this appear to be a game. Nothing could be further from the truth. Smart people do not play games with their career or their personal life. We need to take our lives seriously and also take steps to protect ourselves from the behavior and actions of others. One very effective pro-active way of accomplishing this is to have people ready and willing to take our side and provide support whenever it's needed.

Before we end this chapter, there is one more important aspect of aligning yourself with others that we need to discuss.

This method only works when you are able to instill the right feelings in the minds of others. If you are the person who is always honest and willing to help at work, or if you are the friend that is always supportive and helpful, then this approach will work.

But if you have shown a touch of dishonest behavior in the past, or if you have done a few not so nice things to others, then this strategy could easily fail miserably. The last thing you need is for someone to say "Well, last year he took credit for something that Tom had worked a lot on so I guess he might have done this as well." Or having a friend say to your girlfriend or boyfriend "Look, I don't know if he did this or not but he's done the same type of thing in the past so just watch out."

Getting a response like that is almost as bad as saying "He did it!"

The point I am trying to make is that sometimes your support and reputation are going to be your primary weapons when it comes to defending yourself against a difficult person. Don't do anything that will jeopardize either of those things. Even one guilty act can easily destroy years of reputation building and plant seeds of doubt in the minds of others.

So just do the right thing, inspire confidence and respect and you will be well on your way in protecting yourself against the actions of others.

Market Yourself

Some people depend on others not to promote themselves or their accomplishments. They love the person who quietly goes through their day accomplishing tasks, achieving their goals but never saying a word. It makes them an easy target.

It is amusing to see how some people feel that it is wrong to mention their accomplishments or claim credit for a job well done. They feel it is somehow wrong or will be interpreted as bragging of some sort. While in some cases that might be true, the fact remains that everyone needs to demonstrate their worth both in their personal lives and at work.

Now I am not saying that you should brag about every little thing you do. That act gets old really quick. But if your efforts lead to some kind of major accomplishment, make sure someone knows about it. Sometimes this is easy because everyone will know you were working on something so when it is finished people will know that the results were yours.

But sometimes there are times when you might discover a problem and take care of it without anyone else knowing about it. Sometimes these problems can save the company a ton or money, makes a product better, or makes life easier. If you were responsible for the improvement, someone should know.

Now I am not telling you to brag about what you have done or stand up on your desk and shout out how great you are. That type of response will likely get you severely beaten or your food in the refrigerator tampered with. Instead, let others know of your accomplishments in discrete ways.

For example, if you discovered a defect in the company inventory program and you fixed it, you could go to your boss and say "Tim, I just wanted to let you know that I found a bug in the inventory software that was throwing our counts off. I fixed it and adjusted the counts so it won't be a problem in the future."

That allows you to make someone aware of what you did without saying "Hey! Look what I did!" This is a very effective way of making people aware of what you have done. Just use it at the appropriate time for significant or major situations. It would not be appropriate to say "Hey boss, just noticed the toilet paper in stall 3 was running low so I called building maintenance". Some things are just better left unsaid.

It is important for you to market yourself for several reasons.

The first reason is that your accomplishments and success lead to setting your overall value in the eyes of others. If you do something that benefits others, that should increase your perceived worth. But if no one else is aware that it was you who did it, then you values doesn't increase.

Second, sometimes people in upper management or just management in general are somewhat isolated from the day to day activities. They might be aware that something has been completed or accomplished but have no idea who actually was responsible.

Third, there are people out there who just love to take credit for stuff they didn't do. If they see something done but no one taking the credit, then BOOM! That's something they can grab for themselves! We all have worked with at least one person who either takes credit for things that others have done or inflates their own value through bogus accomplishments.

When people do falsely inflate their own worth, two things can happen. They look better while others look worse. It's like standing in a row of people and one person steps forward. Now he looks ahead while everyone else appears behind. Don't appear behind.

The more people are aware of what you do and what your successes are the stronger and more valuable you appear in their eyes. This helps you whenever something negative might appear.

For example, if your boss is aware of everything you do and the time for a layoff should come, you would be among the last to go. But if you were the type of just quietly went about their job letting others take all the credit, then you might be the first one out the door!

But this is also a double edged sword in that some kind of difficult people will target the best people or the most respected for two reasons. The first is to knock them down a peg or two out of jealousy. The second reason is if you wanted to look better than someone, wouldn't you rather look better than the best person or the worst? My money is on the best person.

Society has changed over the last few decades and it has become more of a "me first" type of mentality. You cannot expect others to shout your praises or advance your career. You need to self promote but you need to do it properly.

As we said, promote yourself discretely so you don't alienate other people. No co-worker likes to be shown up and no friend likes to be made smaller by another friend. Don't be obvious and don't be overbearing.

But do take credit, or allow credit to be given to you, for a job well done or an important achievement. Always remember this: If you do something but no one knows about it, then has it really done you any good?

One last thing. Sometimes you might want to do something without getting or taking any credit. Maybe you do something to help another person and don't want them to know. Or maybe you help someone in need and don't want them to feel embarrassed. Whatever the reason, some things are left unsaid and the satisfaction they bring you kept private.

No one likes a braggart but no one likes to have their work or efforts stolen either. It can be a fine line at times but walk it and walk it carefully.

Show Some Compassion

Difficult people are difficult for a reason. No one is difficult on purpose unless it is just their nature. Fortunately, that represents just a fraction of the people we come in contact with during a normal day.

People are a reflection of their lives and past experiences. So a person might be difficult because they were hurt or abused or taken advantage of earlier in their lives. So they adopt an "I'll get them before they get me" mentality. Though this is not a rational response for you or me, if you have been hurt before this is your protection mechanism.

Another reason someone might be very difficult to work with or interact with is because they are going through some tough times in their lives and their patience and tolerance are almost completely gone. Their thoughts might be somewhere else instead of where they need to be. This is not mean to be an excuse but rather a reason for their behavior.

While this is not a valid reason to hurt or abuse another human being, it does explain the reasons behind the behavior. The good thing about people like this is when you take the reasons away, they become easier to deal with. This is unlike the difficult person who is just difficult because of their personal agenda or just because they enjoy it.

Though it might seem counter intuitive or downright foolish, you might want to step back and show some compassion towards this person until you understand any possible reasons why they are acting this way. Ask around the office or inquire through friends to find out if there are any problems or events going on in that person's life.

Don't be quick to judge or report someone or take serious action until you are more aware of what's really going on. They might have a medical or health issue of their own or a family member. They might have problems with one of their children or financial worries or lord knows what else. Again, while this does not excuse the behavior, it does somewhat explain it.

I think we all owe each other a certain amount of compassion and understanding. Just because your life might be free of trouble or problems does not mean another person has the same lifestyle. We should at least try and understand and possibly cut that person a little bit of slack during these times.

You might even want to help them or at least offer to help. That alone might be enough for the person's attitude to crack and become a little bit better.

This is not about what is right or wrong but rather what gets results.

Sure offering to help or showing compassion might lead to you getting taken advantage of for a while but always consider there just might be a legitimate reason for the behavior. This is especially true if you noticed behavioral changes in someone. If a person who used to be nice, friendly and helpful has suddenly turned nasty and vindictive, there could be a very good reason for that change. So cut that person some slack until you find out why.

This does not mean that you shouldn't be careful. Do not give the other person the benefit of the doubt if that means placing you or others in dangerous situations. After all, your health, safety and future should be of paramount importance to you. But if someone starts acting nasty and turning stuff in late, that's one thing. That might deserve some slack. But if someone starts lashing out and assaulting people, that should be reported and dealt with immediately.

It is the nature of some people to keep troubles and problems inside and never let them come to the surface. It is only after something happens that we find out what that person was going through. Then we feel bad about the things we said or thought during those times.

Sometimes a little compassion, carefully and thoughtfully given can work wonders. It costs us little in time and effort to do this and the possible benefits are huge.

So the next time someone is being difficult with you, take a moment to consider why they are acting that way.

Maybe, just maybe, you can make a difference and turn that attitude around.

Separate the Issue from the Person!

Be completely honest with me. Don't you treat things differently depending on the people who are involved? Don't you take more abuse or negativity from friends and people you like than you do when difficult or adversarial people are concerned?

Of course you do. You are only human.

We all include our feelings about the people involved in our evaluation of what is going on. If people we dislike are involved we are usually more apt to declare them guilty or responsible. If people we like and respect are involved, we usually will reserve judgment, even support them, until the facts prove otherwise.

Perception plays a huge role in most people's decision making. We sometimes look at something at the surface level and make quick decisions based on perception rather than reality. In fact, for a lot of people, perception IS their reality. While this is not fair, it is how the world turns and we need to accept that.

We don't have to agree or support it but we do need to acknowledge it.

That is why it is important to remain objective and allow ourselves some time to step back and gather the truth. We need to replace perception with cold, hard facts. In other words, rather than decide something based on perception, we need to decide based on the truth.

We mentioned reputation and passed history before and how it helps change the way we look at things. It is the way our brain deals with things in order to protect us from harm and negative situations. It is part of our decision making process.

For example, if you have a friend that took your last 4 girlfriends away from you and you heard a rumor that he was seeing your current girlfriend, you would be likely to give that rumor some credibility. Not because you actually saw them dating or caught them in the act, but because that same person did the same thing to you multiple times before.

In the workplace, suppose a co-worker in the past had made mistakes and then placed your name on the paperwork so you would get the blame. If someone did that to you now and he was one of the people who might have done it, wouldn't he be your first suspect? Not because he really did it, but because he had done it in the past

This is normal human behavior even though it can lead to false accusations and false disciplinary action against innocent people.

It is something that some people will count on to get away with something they did because they knew someone else would get the blame first.

Though it might be hard, look for the facts. Don't judge people on their past acts or their personality. You might want to factor those things in when you have facts that support that conclusion but never make total judgment based on rumors or mere suspicion.

That is not to say that you don't take steps to protect yourself and others from the person until the final determination has been made. You would be foolish to lace you life or career in someone's hands that you suspect is doing bad things to you or causing you harm or stress. In other words, protect yourself but don't judge.

Avoid Making Snap Judgments

This is an extension of the previous chapter so this chapter will be short. Very often we make mistakes and falsely blame or accuse people of doing things because we rush to conclusions. We don't take the time to think or research or get to the bottom of something. That leads to uninformed decisions and that often leads to trouble.

One thing that can easily turn a nice and easy going person into someone really difficult to get along with is to be falsely accused of something they didn't do. That can be a very personal matter and lead to severe consequences and long term suspicion. Some people never recover and wear those scars for the rest of their lives. They turn from trusting people into suspicious and cynical people.

Unless the situation calls for immediate reaction and decisions, it is always better to wait until you have more, or even all, the pertinent information before making your decision.

This will make it far more difficult to make the wrong decision or jump to the wrong conclusion.

The damage that can be made by falsely blaming or accusing someone can last for a very long time. So be careful and get as much information as you possibly can before assigning blame.

For those situations that require split second judgment and action, make the decision as best you can but avoid assigning blame or accusing anyone. Creating stop gap measures to get things rolling while you get more information and assess the situation is the best way to go.

Keep in mind that certain people love to create situations where immediate action is required. They do this to keep people from digging too deep into things and to avoid being blamed for something that really is their fault.

A good rule of thumb is if someone is demanding that you make a decision immediately without obvious good cause that should be something you really want to look into. Very rarely in everyday life do we have things that need to be done that second unless someone dropped the ball earlier. I do agree that these kinds of situations can and do occur but I also say they happen far more often than they should.

Do Not Always Agree!

Have you ever had a situation where you just thought it would be easier to just agree with someone to get everything over with? We have all encountered the people who are so determined to get their own way that they just keep hammering and hammering away until we finally cave in.

The problem is that there is a danger in doing this. There are a lot of people who know from experience the longer they stick to their guns and demand what they want that eventually they will prevail. They just know that people will cave and their demands will be met. It's just a matter of time that's all.

Sometimes it is truly tempting to take the easy way out especially when the downside isn't all that bad. If the downside is trivial, you might just think "What the heck, let's just be done with this" and give in. But when we do this, the person looking to advance their own agenda figures out what it's going to take and how to go about getting what they want for the next time.

Some people learn that the way to get things is to keep insisting and insisting and insisting until they get their own way. Every time they are successful it just confirms that what they thought was true. Every time they fail they may question their approach just a little bit more next time.

The other thing that can happen is that every time someone persists and wins they can get increased credibility from others. That can make it even easier for them to push through their own ideas and agenda next time. Some of the most difficult people are the ones who know how to get their own way and are experienced at doing so.

We have talked about picking your battles and that also applies here but you need to be firm and unyielding when it really counts. Come to meetings well informed and have data and information to back up your viewpoint as well. Your success might not lie with convincing the person insisting on getting their way. It might lie in convincing all the others that you are correct and they are wrong. Information and hard data have a way of doing that with people.

Another aspect of this is standing your ground when you know you are right. Some people will use bullying or high pressure tactics to get you to back down and agree with them. This not only can result in the wrong actions moving forward, but can also lessen your credibility at the same time.

People will often run roughshod over others to ram home their own agenda and then when things don't work out, they will be quick to point out that everyone else agreed with them. If you should raise concerns after the fact they will quickly point out that you agreed with them when it came decision making time.

When this happens you really cannot say that you just agreed so everyone could end the meeting or go home. That makes you look bad as well which is just perfect for the person looking to deflect the blame.

Stick up for what you believe is right and try to enlist the help and support of others as well. Having more support and more supporting information and data will make your job easier. It will also tend to make the difficult people trying to advance their agenda think twice about trying to bully or intimidate you in the future.

It is important to understand that what you do today can, and usually will, have an impact on what happens tomorrow as well. Difficult people and bullies learn from their experiences and will adjust their plans to make them more effective the next time around. The more you let them win the stronger they will become and the more difficult they will make it for you next time.

Stand up for what you believe is right at all times.

Deal With Facts!

Whenever you have to deal with a difficult person, try and eliminate guesswork and conjecture and stick with the facts. People who are trying to advances their own agenda, or who are trying to cause or create trouble will have a difficult time when they are confronted with facts.

It is easier to tell people what you believe to be true but something else entirely when you present solid and irrefutable facts to back up your position. Difficult people want what they want for their own reasons and those reasons are not usually based anywhere in reality.

For example, someone might try and have something done another way to get out of doing the work themselves. Maybe their way involves having another group or department do the work instead of them. So even though it might be the wrong way to proceed, they fight for it because it is much easier for them.

The best way to stop someone dead in their tracks, or at least set them back on their heels a bit, is to understand why your way is the best way and then finding facts and data to support that.

Now this only works when your way IS the better way. If you are trying to push through your way because you want to give the work to someone else then in this case YOU are the difficult person!

You should never try to dispute something someone says with opinions unless you can back them up with fact or a convincing argument. Be prepared to respond to challenges from others but do so in a calm and professional manner. Don't get nasty or go down to their level or take it personally. Just give a clear cut answer that leaves little room for disagreement.

Like this:

Difficult co-worker: I think we should let marketing handle this one. We are way too overworked to handle this right now and they are better prepared to do this sort of thing. (In reality, he wants to slide the work to someone else so he can leave early.)

You: I think we are better trained to do this within our own group where we will have control over the content and direction the company will take. Marketing is more concerned with promoting the product while we are more in tune with supporting it and this project is more support oriented than a marketing issue.

Difficult co-worker: Listen, that's easy for you to say but this is a product issue and should be handled by marketing. Those guys are professionals over there and they would not lead us down the wrong path and they are more prepared for this kind of thing than we are. I still think marketing should handle this.

You: I see your point but I did a little research and I found out that 50% of our issues had to do with marketing claims and marketing issues. To put them in charge of something that is our responsibility to support is not wise. As far as manpower and workload is concerned, I checked with marketing and they are scheduling their people 3 weeks out and we are just one week out. So not only can we do this better we can also do it faster.

Difficult co-worker: I still think they should do it.

You: I understand that but in this case, it seems like the best decision is that we handle this ourselves. We can always go to marketing for assistance and final evaluation if we feel that is necessary.

With this example we refuted the difficult co-workers position not with a direct attack but by backing up our position with clear and easy to understand reasons. We told them not what we thought and why we thought that.

When the co-worker disagreed again and pushed the issue we released more facts to support our position and drove the issue home. We did all of this in a calm and non confrontational manner that did not assess blame or ridicule on anyone.

The beauty of how this ended is that while the co-worker made a weak plea at the end, we made the final decision our way but also said we could include marketing in the final part of the project if necessary.

This gave the difficult person a way off backing off without appearing to have been beaten.

Most of the time rational thought will defeat someone who is just trying to be difficult or advance their own personal agenda. Well presented arguments supported by facts will always win over emotion and opinions. Well, maybe not 100% of the time but pretty darned close.

Document Things

Difficult people are difficult because they make our lives more complicated than they need to be. You cannot deal with difficult people using common sense because often what they are trying to do has nothing whatsoever to do with common sense in the first place.

To make things worse, sometimes we find ourselves having to justify doing something the right way because someone else insists we are or were wrong. The fact that we are not to blame and that someone else is the root of the problem sometimes makes no difference at all.

It is difficult at times to justify a particular course of action or a response to a problem. We may do something or recommend something because of a feeling or emotion and these things do not translate very well into words.

So it is important to document certain things that we do when we are dealing with a significant issue or a difficult person. In business any Human Resource person will tell you that you must have documented examples or studies of things that have happened before you can discipline anyone.

A lawyer will tell you that you have to have specific documented evidence to support your claims against a person as well.

Most of the time we will not be involving lawyers or human resources but we still should be documenting issues that have escalated or continued over long periods of time.

Documentation provides a history of specific examples or situations that support your position against a person or company. Documentation should be as specific and accurate as possible. It should include only facts and it should also contain dates, times and names if applicable.

Documenting things solves a few important problems for us and helps further our efforts. Here are some of the reasons why documenting things can be so important:

Our memories tend to fade over time. So what was so vivid today will be less vivid tomorrow let alone next week or next month. Specific details such as time or sequence may become unclear and actually can help create doubt as to what happened when.

When we document something when it happens or right after, little things that seem unimportant at the time can be written down and might become important later. The little things get lost over time. We can also capture the emotion and circumstances more clearly right away than weeks or months afterward.

Documentation also helps you refer back to make sure your story and version of events is accurate.

It allows you to refresh your memory and keep your version clear and accurate from day to day or meeting to meeting. This can come in very handy if you have meetings where you have to recount what occurred several times. Your documentation can help you say the same thing every time even when those meetings are several months or years apart.

Documentation also makes it very difficult for people to call you a liar or dispute the events as they are portrayed. When someone is confronted with a documents accounting of several incidents or situations, it can take the fight out of them pretty quickly.

This is not always about a win-win victory here but sometimes just being able to squash something right at the start by showing that you are not someone who is easily victimized can help you stop this behavior quickly.

Bullies and other difficult people tend to go where they will meet the least resistance. They will target weaker people or people who do not have the strength or knowledge to go up against them. In other words, they want an easy mark. The last thing they want is a worthy adversary who is going to come back to them with all kinds of documentation and accounts of what they had done in the past or during that incident.

If possible, documentation can also include statements from other people who actually witnessed or experienced the event in question. This way it is actually more than your word against someone else's word.

It because 3 against one or four against one or so on. The more people who support you account of what happened the better is looks for you.

Documentation should consist of facts relevant to the matter at hand. Anything that is not relevant should be excluded so it does not appear that you are out to assassinate the character of the other person. It should not include opinion or conjecture but should stick to what was actually seen or witnessed.

All documentation should be dated and the names of people who were there when the incident happened should be written down as well in case those people need to be contacted at a later date. You never know when that might be necessary.

Documentation might also include photos if any injuries or damage occurred or if there were any visual aspects of the action. For example, if someone sent you an inappropriate or obscene card or letter, taking a picture of it would be evidence that the item did in fact exist. Original can be destroyed by the other person and then no proof might exist.

Pictures of injuries along with any medical reports or hospital bills would also be relevant to indicate the true extent of those injuries.

A few paragraphs before we mentioned lawyers or Human Resources. If the person you are dealing with has done things that bring the dispute to either of those directions, you should consult with Human /resources, or a lawyer, to find out the specific documentation or information that you should be gathering.

Those items will differ from situation to situation. Do not rely strictly on the information in this chapter when it comes to legal or Human Resource issues. Get advice from the respective parties and follow it to the letter.

Now that we have put the fear of the lord into everyone, let's dial this back and discuss the normal day to day issues that you are likely to get involved in. People may ask you to do certain things that you are not supposed to do and they may do this over and over and over again.

Smart people make those requests verbally so there is no record of the request anywhere. When that happens to me, I just ask them to send me a quick e-mail stating the request for my records in case I need to refer to it later. This accomplishes two things. First, it puts the other person on notice that I want a record of the request. Second, it provides a record for me to show to someone else if the person denies asking for that particular task. Usually this will stop that kind of activity dead in its tracks.

Naturally, it is important to store your documentation in a safe place where others cannot get to it and take it or change it. Bring it home with you, keep it in a secure folder on a server but remember that anything on a hard drive will be lost if the hard drive crashes. Someone who knows his or her job is on the line based on what they know is on your PC might be tempted to make sure your PC doesn't work in the morning.

One popular question is "How long should I keep this documentation?

Well, you should consult a lawyer or Human Resources for significant or serious issues but for the most part, documentation today can be stored on a computer hard drive or flash drive or even on a CD-Rom. So space really isn't as big a deal as it used to be. A $5 flash drive can store thousands of pages of information and hundreds of photos.

With that in mind I would keep all information safely stored away and not delete any of it until you are no longer working there or when that person no longer exists in your life. Even then you never know when that person might return or when someone else might come around making that information relevant and valuable again.

So keep all documentation. When and if the flash drive gets full, burn it on a CD or spend another $5 and get another drive. It's cheap insurance for you.

Use I Instead of You

It is amazing how the choice of the words we use can make all the difference in the world when it comes to how they are heard and accepted. When dealing with people who are confrontational or difficult in nature, we must be extra careful in the words we use.

No one likes to be confronted or accused of something even if they are guilty. So, we should try and phrase our statements using non confrontational words. Words that still get the point of our message across to the other people but do so in a non threatening manner.

There are several ways of accomplishing this but probably the easiest way is to make all statements using the word "I" instead of the word "YOU". For example, instead of saying "You didn't submit your part of the project on time and we all suffered." You might say "I notice that your part of the project wasn't submitted on time and that caused us problems". You said pretty much the same thing but in a non confrontational way.

This is even more important when dealing with a group of people. I am a firm believer in handling negative situations individually and in private rather than in a group setting. If someone doesn't like being accused of something one on one, they are going to absolutely hate it if it happens in a group!

Using the previous example, you might handle the individual part in private and use the generic approach like we did above in a group setting. If the person protests or says that wasn't true, well, they have opened the door and the matter can be discussed in a group setting letting the pieces fall where they may.

Using the word "you" at the beginning of a sentence is very direct and might inflame the situation. Though you might not actually stress the word at all in your voice, the other person probably here's a capital YOU instead of the normal you. When people feel threatened or accused, they get defensive and things can rapidly go downhill from that point on.

This is not about hurting people's feelings or singling people out for blame. It is all about making sure the people involved are aware of the problem and their role in it without embarrassing them or minimizing their role in the group.

Also keep in mind that there is little benefit in assessing blame.

You can get the message across without actually assessing blame. Saying," I know your part of the project was submitted late so can we make sure that doesn't happen again?" is a lot easier than saying You submitted your work late and it cost all of us in the project." Both said the same thing but the first way was a kinder and gentler version.

You might be amazed at how positively someone might react to being treated in this manner. Be held up to ridicule might make someone turn combative or it might cause them to pull back and be so self conscious that they never do anything of substance again because they are afraid of making a mistake.

Some of you might say that this is sugar coating incompetence and allowing people to continue doing sub standard work or put in a below average effort. Contrary to what you might think, that is exactly 100% wrong.

There is a big difference treating people with respect and making an example out of them. If someone does something the first time, possibly even the second time, handle it with reservation and class. Be respectful of the person and handle matters privately. This shows your consideration for other people. Most people will appreciate that and respond in a positive manner.

But, if the behavior continues, then you can escalate your response to include bringing it up in front of the group to show that you mean business and that you have no intention of allowing behavior detrimental to others to continue.

It always ceases to amaze me that some people, after being given chance after chance, still get mad when they are confronted in front of others. I mean, you had a bunch of chances and still continued the same behavior! Did you think you would continue to be given more chances to screw up????

This entire process falls in line with something we already discussed. That is treating people with dignity and respect. People want to be treated in that manner. They respect people who treat them with respect. The thing most people do not get is that you don't command respect, you earn it.

People don't respect you because they have to; they respect you because they want to. So the next time someone is difficult to deal with or causes you problems, take the non-confrontational approach when dealing with that person. Give them every opportunity to turn their attitude and performance around.

It's not important that you assess blame, it is important that you improve results.

It's not important to be the winner; it's about improving the results.

It's not about being stronger; it's about improving the results.

For those who have not got it yet, it's the results that matter, not blaming someone in the process.

Express Appreciation When Deserved

I don't care who you are or how important you are. I don't care if you are the CEO or the janitor. If someone does something for you or something that helps you out, express your appreciation. That goes a long way.

A lot of people today feel that they should go through life having things done for them without showing or expressing their appreciation. They just take and take and never think about saying thank you or just telling someone they did a good job.

I actually worked for a boss who told me that they pay our salaries so they don't have to say thank you. Our pay said thanks for them. Excuse me but that's a giant pile of crap. Granted, money is a type of reward but it does not eliminate the need for common courtesy or expressing gratitude.

People get frustrated when they do great work or achieve great things and no one says anything. They start to feel taken for granted or unappreciated.

When this happens they become disenchanted and unhappy. And when that happens, many people become, you guessed it:
Difficult

So make an effort to show appreciation and thanks to people who do the right thing or people who support you or work for you. Thank your friends for their contributions to your life and thank you spouse for his or her support as well.

There are far too many people in this world who go through life thinking that people owe them something just because they are here on this earth. Don't be one of those people. Show appreciation, show that you care and let people know that you are aware of what they have done for you.

In my life I always make an effort to tell people I appreciate what they have done for me. The result of doing that has paid me dividends over and over. Although that is not why I do it, my efforts have resulted in people wanting to do more for me. Not having to do more but wanting to do more. There's a big difference.

I once was in a meeting when a national Manager told us the people should feel obligated to do a good job for us because we pay them to. My first thought was "This guy just doesn't get it." People should do a good job not because they feel obligated to; they should do it because they want to.

If you show appreciation to people they will most often respond favorably to you and act more positive towards you as well.

Difficult people who are that way because they had trouble with people in the past might view you with suspicion at first but once they see you are sincere, you can watch the walls come down and they just might not be so difficult moving forward.

People often wonder how I get so much accomplished when I have just a few resources at my disposal. The fact is that the way I treat people makes them want to do a better job for me. I have people who always look for a better way to get things done even without my asking. Not only does this make my job and life easier, it makes me feel good knowing these people do this for me without asking.

Whenever possible, I try and take this one step further. Without giving a reason and without it being a special occasion I will send someone who works for me a small gift. Maybe it's a $100 gift card or a certificate for a dinner at a nice restaurant. I enclose a note with it saying "Just wanted to say thanks for doing a great job for me. I appreciate it."

Now $100 isn't going to break me and it isn't going to make a world of difference to the person receiving the gift card. But the sentiment behind it and how the people feel when they receive it gets me back several times that $100 in increased performance and attitude.

I t just makes sense. People do better and perform at higher levels when they feel appreciated and when they are recognized for their efforts. It's not the size of the gift that matters. It is the thought and appreciation behind it.

I even know of one person who never cashed in his $100 certificate. He keeps it in his office and looks at it from time to time just to remind himself that his efforts are important and appreciated. He uses that certificate as a reminder to help keep him focused and engaged in what he is doing.

So the next time you meet or interact with someone who doesn't seem to want to be part of a positive effort, find something to thank him for. When he does a good job recognize his efforts. When something he is involved in experiences a success, recognize his part of it.

It is amazing how much a little positive reinforcement can go when given at the right time for the right reason.

Why not give it a chance. You have little to lose and a whole lot to gain.

Provide People with an Escape Route

No one likes to be wrong. Even fewer people like to be proven wrong. And absolutely no one likes being boxed into a corner where every option is a negative one. In fact, if you want to get more out of people with a minimum of stress and a far greater chance of success in the future, give people a way out of a situation that works for them.

As we said a few times already, it is not so much assessing or placing blame as it is to improve the results and eliminate those same problems in the future. So if I change a person's behavior without blaming them or making them feel like they lost, then everyone wins.

A lot of difficult people are difficult because they do not like to lose or have others know that they lost. Whether it is pride or just the feeling of possible embarrassment, no one likes to admit defeat. But if you can find a way to have someone lose without appearing to lose, you will have a much better chance of success.

Sometimes you will find yourself in a situation where you know you are 100% right and even your opponent realizes that as well. But they keep arguing or fighting because they do not want to admit defeat publicly. Admitting defeat hurts their pride and can be embarrassing as well.

But what if there was a way where they could change their mind, agree with you but still not admit defeat? Do you think more people would agree with you then? Of course they would. When you can take the guilt or embarrassment out of the equation a lot more people will change their views and vote with you.

For example, if you want something to go one way and another person wants it to go in a different direction, you could say something like "Look, all the data and research support my plan and nothing indicates anything at all like what you are proposing." That sums it up but it makes the other person appear to be wrong and ineffective.

Contrast that with this statement:

"Look, all the data seems to support my position and the research supports the data as well. After looking at everything I can easily see why someone might think the best way to go was your way but looking deeper I found that wasn't always the best choice."

You still made the same point but you added some comments that seemed to indicate it was a legitimate error that could have been made by anyone.

With that one statement you took the pressure off and you significantly reduced the negative feelings of the other person. The other person can now use that comment, take it one step further and say something like "After looking at what Bob said, I understand why he feels the way he does and now feel comfortable heading in the direction he wants to go."

The result is that you get his "buy in" and he gets to keep his dignity at the same time. It always pays to allow people to exit a situation with their dignity and pride intact. We should concentrate only on results and long term benefits. Again, this is not about winning or assessing blame. This IS about getting things done right and improving relationships between people.

Another useful phrase I use with great success is "I have seen this happen many times in the past when......." This lets people know they were not stupid and their error was a common one. Whether this is actually true or not remains to be seen but it allows people to be told they made a mistake without making them feel bad.

So the next time you find yourself in a situation where a decision must be made, ask yourself two questions. The first question should be "Which way is the very best way to go and why?" the second question should be "How can I make it easier for the other people to change their mind and join our side?"

If you can ask yourself and answer those questions correctly, you will find yourself on the receiving end of a lot more success!

Learn to Ignore

Sometimes there are people who are difficult to get along with but really don't do that much harm. IN fact, you might say these people are far more annoying than they are difficult. But they still cause you grief and they still introduce stress in your life. So what do you do with these people?

Obviously your first choice would be to remove them from your life if they provide no other benefit to you. If one of your friends just becomes over the top annoying and offers nothing to make you enjoy or need their company, you can just part ways. People who are dating and no longer feel any attachment for each other do this all the time.

But what do you do when you can't remove them from your life? Maybe it's a co-worker that you have to interact with but you don't want to get a new job and there is no ability to transfer and you haven't hit the lottery yet.

Maybe it's a family member who is just annoying and short of whacking them in their sleep, you just have to continue to deal with them. Whatever the set of circumstances might be, let's just say you have no choice but to continue to deal with them. What do you do?

Learn to ignore them.

Learn to adapt to the situation so that whatever it is they do that makes them so annoying it no longer bothers you. This is not always as simple as it sounds but humans have a way of gradually adapting and getting used to things. Eventually they don't notice the distractions or annoying behavior.

If someone has an annoying habit that bugs you, distract yourself from it whenever possible. If someone hums all day long, consider getting some headphones or earplugs so you don't hear it.

If someone is constantly talking to you while you are trying to work, politely tell them you prefer to have personal conversations during breaks because you are trying to concentrate.

We cannot control the actions and personalities of others. But we can control our reactions. We can learn to become more tolerant and to let little things roll off our backs and no longer create problems.

As I stated this is not always as easy as it sounds. But some of us are far too intolerant in this world and sometimes, just sometimes, the problem doesn't lie with the other person, it lies within us. When that is the case we need to lighten up.

Of course, when the offending behavior starts to become unbearable or abusive, we should enlist the help of others or make changes to limit the exposure to that behavior. Whether this occurs in a work environment or in our personal lives, we always need to balance things and determine what is more important and what needs to be acted upon.

Escalate When Needed

There will be times when dealing with difficult people will become something that is more difficult than one person can handle. It is during these times when we have to get others involved and seek outside assistance in dealing with those people. This should not be considered a sign of weakness or failure. Instead, it should be looked at as an act of strength and wisdom. Knowing one's limitations is a very important and valuable skill.

Whenever something or someone becomes too much for you to handle, you should escalate the issue and seek outside help or assistance. In the workplace, that help might come from a co-worker, your boss, or possibly Human Resources. In your personal life help might come from a spouse, family member or friend. In extreme cases the help might come from a lawyer or the police.

Wherever the help comes from it is important that you seek it out when you need it.

Sometimes difficult people plan things in such a way that the efforts of one person just are not effective. Keep in mind people who want to hurt or annoy you are not going to figure out something that is easy for you to combat. They are going to make things as difficult as possible. Not everyone will do this but some absolutely will.

Usually problems or issues in the workplace have a well defined escalation structure. If you have a problem you report it to your manager or supervisors and they either deal with it on their level or they direct you to the next step. That might be human resources. They might even escalate the issue for you depending on the company policy.

Personal lives are a lot different. There is no manager (unless you are married but that's the topic for another book…) or supervisor to go to for help. The good news is that almost everyone has some kind of support structure already in their lives that they can turn to for help. That might be a friend or relative of even someone at work.

Even when you don't really need help but are unsure of what to do or how to act, enlisting the opinions of others can add a different and important perspective on things. We are all different and we all look at the same situation and see different things. Sometimes another person can point out something that should have been obvious but you somehow missed. Since the more information the better, running something past someone else is almost always a good thing.

Sometimes the behavior or situation involves more than one person or "victim". In these cases, the people involved might want to get together and discuss what they can do as part of a group to resolve the situation. There is a saying that goes something like "There is strength in numbers" and that is very true when it comes to stopping bad or negative behavior. Especially in the workplace.

Any time more than one person comes to someone with the same problem, people are more likely to listen. At the Human Resource level, for example, one person coming in with a complaint might not get acted on without concrete evidence because there are legal issues involved and a burden of proof that has to be met before action can be taken. If it is just you coming forward, it could be your word against the other person. And guess what? They are not likely to say "Oh, yeah. I did it. My bad." They are going to say you are wrong or that it is you with the problem.

But when 3 or 4 people go to Human Resources all with similar complaints against the same person, people will listen. That is because there is more evidence involved and more credibility.

We have just discussed the need to document and when you escalate something it is always good to have some kind of documentation to support your claim. This does not mean that if you have no documentation that you cannot escalate something. It is just better to have supporting facts to back up your claims.

There is one issue that you should be aware of before you escalate a problem. This is not intended to convince you to not escalate. It is just intended to make you aware of everything so you can make the best decision possible.

Once you escalate or get other people involved, you kind of can't go back. The issue is no longer a private issue between you and someone else. You now have others involved and you lose the ability to work things out privately. Because of this, it is advisable to try and resolve things locally first and exhaust those possibilities. This allows you to resolve things without anyone getting in trouble or facing discipline.

In a lot of cases, people are going to be far more willing to stop if they can avoid trouble or the possibility of trouble. In fact, some people cause trouble to see how much they can get away with or how much a person can take. Once they know, they back off. This is not rational behavior but then again, difficult people are not rational people.

But if you escalate something, you are committed to go through until the end and that means the other person is going to be forced to either admit to the behavior or fight. At this point there is no backing off without guilt. Many difficult people will fight back and fight back hard. You need to be prepared for this.

The only time it might not be prudent to try and resolve something locally is when the behavior or the damage is so great or involves physical violence or safety.

For example, if someone corners you and molests you at work or in a store, you don't sit down with them for a cup of coffee and try and resolve it privately. You go straight to your boss, Human Resources or the authorities and have them handle it. You do NOT put yourself in harm's way trying to reason with a violent person!

But the reality is that the vast majority of situations or behavior you will encounter will not be at that level. It will be office politics, hidden agendas and people trying to get ahead at your expense that you will encounter. In those cases, trying to resolve it privately at first is usually the best plan of action.

Focus on what YOU Can do to Make Things Better!

Whenever more than one person is involved in anything, the possibility of friction and trouble exists. While there are things we can do to minimize these occurrences, there is nothing we can do to eliminate them. No two people are exactly alike and no two people are going to agree on everything all the time. We just have to accept that.

There will also be times when things happen that are totally out of our control. There will always be times when you have to deal with something you couldn't prevent or that you didn't even see coming. That does not mean you did anything wrong, it just means you are human.

We can go crazy trying to control things we just have no control over. We can worry about this and that even though we have nothing to do with these things.

This can increase our stress levels and make a difficult person or situation even more difficult. So we need to change the way we approach certain things. I'm going to make it a little easier for you to do that. I'm going to give you one simple plan of action that will help you deal with situations better and more effectively.

From this point on, I want you to concentrate only on those things that you have at least some control over. I don't want you to worry about what this person might do or what that person might say. Those people are counting on you doing that because that is what they want to see happen. When this happens they are able to negatively effect your life without actually DOING anything!

You can't complain to someone else because you think someone is going to do something unless you have specific evidence. You can't go to Human Resources and tell them you think a co-worker is plotting something against you or that they are looking at you funny.

Instead, concentrate on what YOU can do to take control over your feelings and the situation. If you feel someone is planning on doing something against you, then align yourself with others so you will be protected and have witnesses. Don't worry about what might be, protect yourself against it.

If you are involved in a negative situation don't hope that the other person will make things better. Concentrate on what YOU can do to make things better. IN every situation one person has to make the first move.

If you are concerned primarily about getting the best results, you will make that first move.

We have little to no control over what someone else does. But we have an almost unlimited control over what we do. We have choices to make and options to consider. Usually there is something WE can do to make things better. Maybe we talk to the person or maybe we escalate the situation to the next level.

Maybe it means we need to start documenting things as they happen to build a case against the offending party. Whatever it is that we plan to do; we should concern ourselves primarily with what we can do to make things better.

We mentioned earlier in this book that if you change nothing, nothing changes. So if you keep doing the same thing and the other person keeps doing what they are doing, things will not get better. They will likely get worse.

The worse things get the more difficult they become to resolve. Feelings get hurt more, anger is higher, and the damages done only get worse and worse as time goes by. Instead of worrying about what might happen, concentrate on what you can do to prevent it.

Take responsibility for your actions and let someone else worry about theirs.

What Was YOUR Role?

I saved this one for last because I did not want
anyone to get upset and throw this book into
the fireplace or gas grille. But what I have to talk
about here is very important and just has to be
said.

When we encounter a difficult person or a
difficult situation, we always need to consider
that maybe, just maybe, that we have some role
in the problem. I'm not saying we do, but we
need to at least consider it.

Look, personalities sometimes clash and it is
not all one person's fault. Maybe you are
reading something into the situation that really
isn't there or maybe you are just being too
sensitive. It's not that you are doing anything
wrong, you are just contributing to the problem
in some way that you are not aware of.

Every story and situation has two sides.
Sometimes, in the case of a bully, one person is
at fault. But sometimes there are disagreements
because one person said or did something the
other person didn't like or there is history
between the two parties.

Before you take any action you should see if there is anything you did that played a role in the situation or if there is anything that you did, or can do, that would make things better. If you can come up with anything, make some changes and see if that improves things a bit.

In order for situations to get resolved, everyone must take responsibility for their actions. No one is immune from this. So take responsibility for the things you have done, if any, and then move on. Do not think that you are effect because no one is.

There are can any number of reasons why situations happen. But we cannot, and should not, discount the fact that we might have contributed in some way to the problem. I'm not saying you did, just that you should consider the possibility.

Now please go and take this book out of the fireplace.

Have a Reason for Everything That You Do!

This last chapter is one that contains the only generic lesson in the whole book. This lesson will, or at least should, work in every situation with almost every person. Not only in business or at home and not only with difficult people. It works even better with "normal" folks as well.

The one thing everyone should remember is that there should be a reason behind everything that you do. In other words, you should understand why you are want to do something before you do it. You should never act first and think later unless the situation demands it.

The reasons should be good ones at the time and it is not all that important if they are shown to be poor reasons after the fact. No one makes the right decisions all the time and everyone makes mistakes. But there should be good reasons why you do something in order for you to do it in the first place.

You never want to say "I don't know." When someone asks you why you did what you did or made that decision. You should be able to understand your thought process at the time and be able to explain it to others. Very often something that appears to be stupid or foolish after the fact had some pretty good reasoning behind it in the beginning.

Now that we agree that we should have reasons for doing what we do, let's take it one step further and add one last criteria to the equation.

Everything that we do should be done in order to make something better. Not to make it worse or to allow it to stay the same, unless that is our desired result. We should be focusing our efforts on doing positive things that bring situations closer to a resolution.

So when you decide to do something, ask yourself "How is this going to make things better?" and also "Is there any way this could make things worse?" If you ask those questions and come up with the right answers, you stand a good chance of making everything better and not more complicated.

This is not a complicated process. We are not talking about hours and hours or days of thinking here. We are talking about a few minutes. We are talking about putting a couple of safeguards in place that require you to think things through just a bit before acting. We are talking about thinking about the repercussions involved in our actions and making reasonably sure what we are about to do is right.

Most of the time we will go ahead with our original plans anyway because they were based on informed decisions. But there will also be time when we might "tweak" things just a bit because we discovered a possible negative or two in our thinking.

Is this going to make us perfect? Hell, no. we will still make mistakes.

But the more we think about what we are doing before we act the higher our level of understanding is likely to be and the more we will learn from our mistakes.

Everyone makes mistakes. It's just that some of us learn from our mistakes and don't repeat them while others keep making the same mistakes over and over again.

It is up to you to decide which person do you want to be? Do you want to be the person who takes time to make reasonably sure their decisions are sound? Or do you want to be the person who acts impulsively and hopes for the best?

It's a really easy decision to make. I hope you make the right one.

Conclusion

After reading this book I hope you have a better understanding of how to interact with difficult people. I hope you understand that communication is one of your strongest and most important weapons. I also hope you understand that you should not stand by and let yourself be the target or any form of abuse.

We all have a responsibility to protect ourselves, and sometimes others, from abuse and negative behavior. It is never right to turn away from abuse whether it is directed at you or someone else. It is also never correct to allow people to continue to take advantage of others as well.

I hope your better understanding of the subject empowers you to take more focused and more effective action whenever it's needed. If it does fulfill that purpose then the effort and time required to write this book has been more than worth it.

It is also important to understand that everyone has an obligation to make this world a better place in which to work, live and love. We cannot stand by and watch other people ruin lives or abuse other people. We need to stand up and be counted when it counts.

You have already taken the first step by acknowledging that something needs to be done and trying to learn how to go about doing it. I commend you for taking that first step.

Keep this book around as a reference and refer back to it whenever you feel the need. It will always be there for you to help guide you down the right path.

If you would like more information on this and other Office Skills manuals and resources, please visit our website at:

http://www.infowhse.com

Be sure to sign up for our newsletter And receive a FREE E-book when you do!

23825091R00081

Printed in Great Britain
by Amazon